# FIRE

## BY STEWART ROSS

# TULIP BOOKS®

Text by Stewart Ross in cooperation with Christine Clover.
© copyright in this edition Tulip Books 2019

The right of the Author to be identified as the Author of this work
has been asserted by the Author in accordance with the Copyright,
Designs and Patents Act 1988.

Printed by Melita

ISBN 978-1-78388-125-3

# Index

# Always there

Fire has been with us from the beginning.

« When our world was formed, it was a **ball of fire**.

Fire is in nature.

We see it in erupting volcanoes and in wild fires started by lightning.

# Taking control

Thousands of years ago, people learned to control wild fire.

## WOW!

When two pieces of wood are rubbed together very fast, they catch fire.

They put it in a **hearth** for cooking and keeping warm.

« Later, they learned to make their own fire. They did this with **friction**.

# Using fire

Fire gave out heat in cold weather and scared away dangerous wild animals.

**WOW!**
Striking flint and steel together makes sparks for starting a fire.

Food cooked on a fire tasted better, too. Fire was also used to clear woodland for farming. »

# Fighting with fire

Human beings learned to use fire in war. They shot fire arrows from bows.

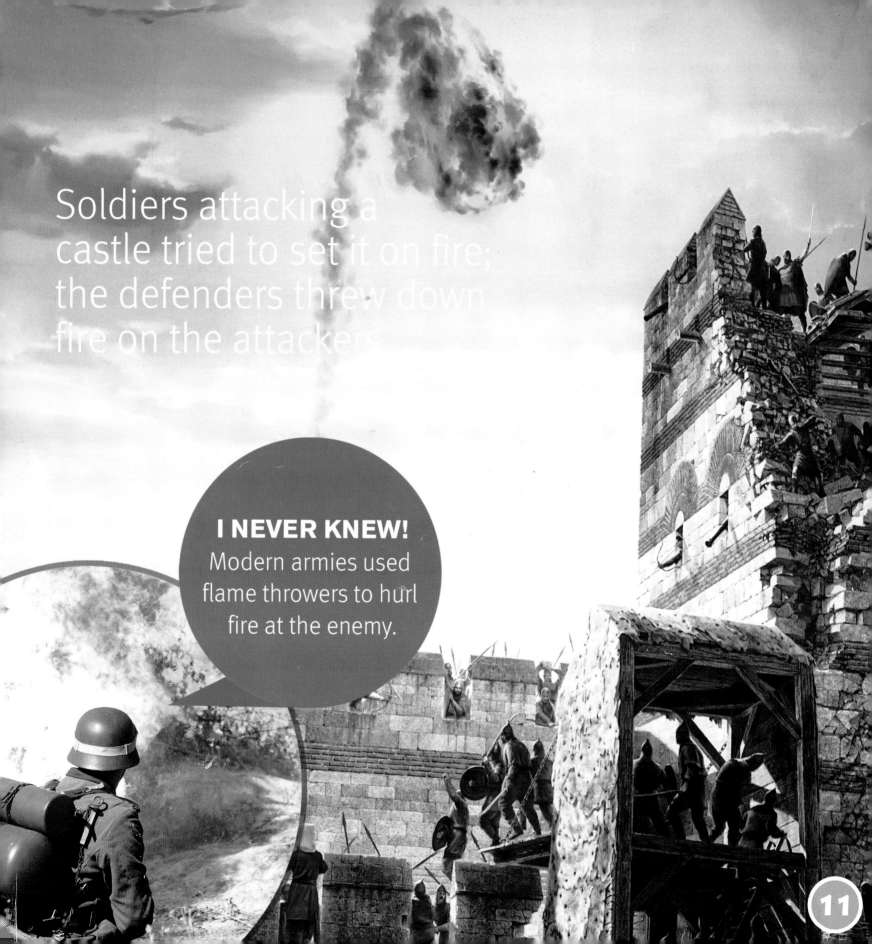

Soldiers attacking a
castle tried to set it on fire;
the defenders threw down
fire on the attackers.

**I NEVER KNEW!**
Modern armies used
flame throwers to hurl
fire at the enemy.

# The chemistry of fire

When **oxygen** mixes with another substance, we call the process **oxidation**.

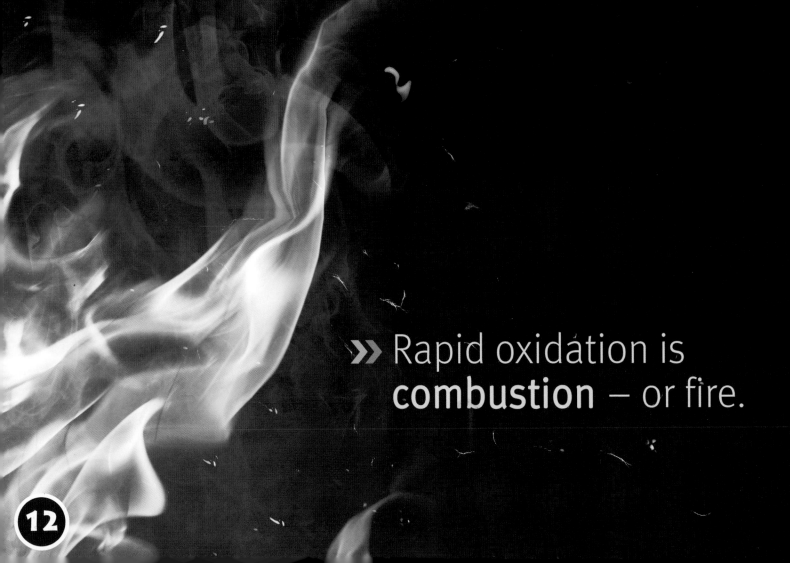

» Rapid oxidation is **combustion** – or fire.

Combustion produces heat, light and gasses. The popular name for these gasses is smoke.

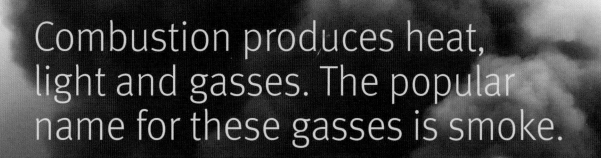

**I NEVER KNEW!**
Oxygen combines slowly with iron to produce rust.

# Fire power – steam

Cooks had always used fire to boil water. The water **expanded** into **steam**.

This **expansion** happened with great force.

**I NEVER KNEW!**
Coal, the fuel used for the first steam engines, is a rock formed from dead trees and plants!

In modern times, engineers used this force to drive **steam engines** and **steam turbines**.

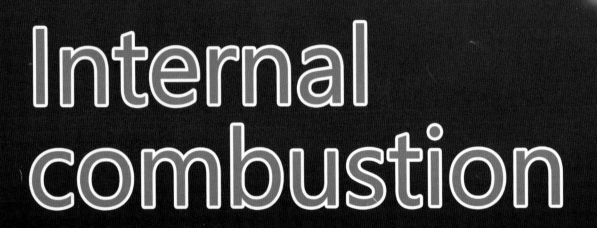

# Internal combustion

The gasses from combustion expand. Their **volume** is greater than that of the oxygen and fuel.

Over 200 years ago, engineers started using this power of expansion to make the internal combustion engine.

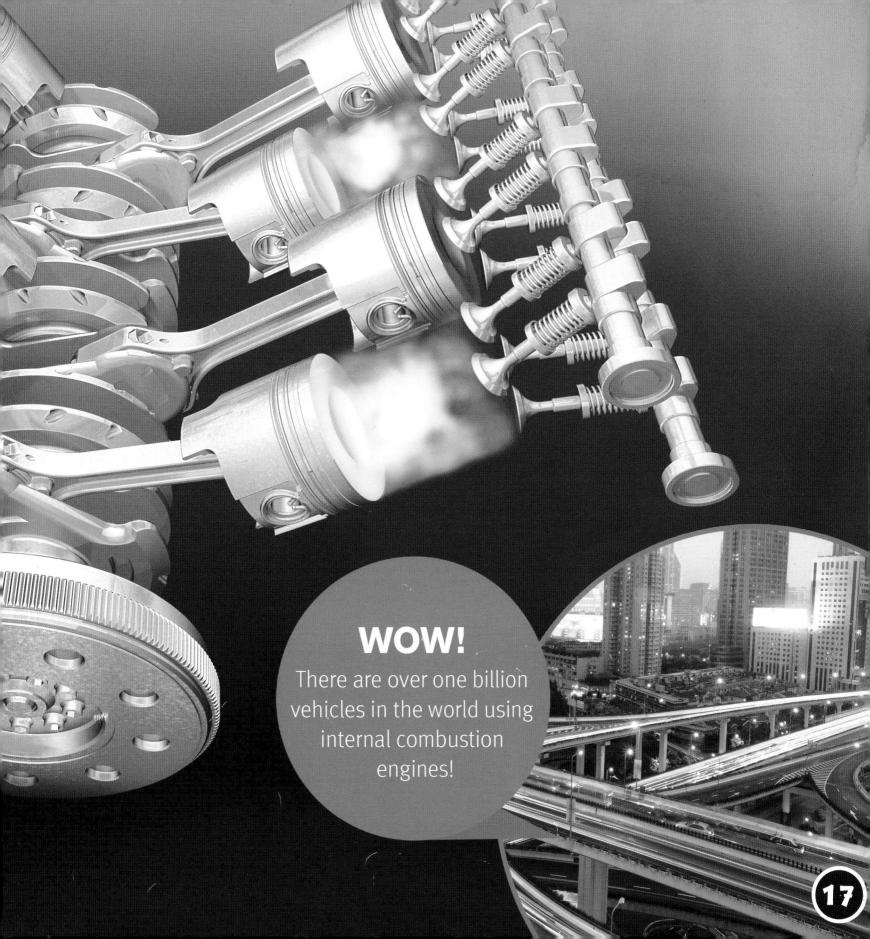

## WOW!

There are over one billion vehicles in the world using internal combustion engines!

# Jets and rockets

Fire also powers **jet** engines.

The combustion of liquid fuel and air produces hot gasses.

These gasses shoot out of the back of a jet engine, thrusting it forward with great power.

**I NEVER KNEW!**
Rocket engines burn liquid oxygen rather than air.

# Fire fighting

Fire is extremely dangerous.
It destroys buildings and even whole towns.

Fire can be put out (extinguished) by:

- Cutting off its oxygen supply, or
- Lowering the temperature so combustion stops.

**I NEVER KNEW!**

A small fire extinguisher normally contains water or a **chemical** (liquid or foam).

# Our dangerous friend

Burning carbon (wood, coal, oil) produces the gas **carbon dioxide**.

It rises into the **atmosphere**, trapping the Sun's heat around the Earth.

**WOW!**
Because of global warming the ice around the North Pole is shrinking fast. It may even disappear!

This **global warming** changes our climate, making life harder for plants and animals.

# Glossary

**Atmosphere**
The gasses (mainly oxygen, nitrogen and carbon dioxide) around the Earth.

**Carbon dioxide**
A colourless gas consisting of atoms of oxygen and carbon.

**Chemical**
A man-made substance.

**Expand**
Increase in size or volume.

**Flint**
A hard, sharp stone.

**Friction**
Heat produced by rubbing together two materials.

**Hearth**
Place where an open fire is lit for cooking or heating.

**Internal combustion engine**
An engine powered by fuel burning in a small space; used in most modern vehicles.

**Oxidation**
The process whereby a substance combines with oxygen.

**Oxygen**
A basic element needed for life – and fire.

**Steam**
Water vapour.

**Steam engine**
An engine driven by the power of water turning to steam.

**Steam turbine**
An engine driven by a jet of steam hitting a fan.

**Volume**
The amount of space taken up by something.